HAL•LEONARD
INSTRUMENTAL
PLAY-ALONG

AUDIO
ACCESS
INCLUDED

PLAYBACK+
Speed • Pitch • Balance • Loop

FLUTE

THE BEATLES

Cover Photo: Fiona Adams/Getty

To access audio visit:
www.halleonard.com/mylibrary

6246-9021-1613-6660

Audio Arrangements by Peter Deneff

ISBN 978-1-4950-9066-0

7777 W. BLUEMOUND RD. P.O. BOX 13819 MILWAUKEE, WI 53213

In Australia Contact:
Hal Leonard Australia Pty. Ltd.
4 Lentara Court
Cheltenham, Victoria, 3192 Australia
Email: ausadmin@halleonard.com.au

Visit Hal Leonard Online at
www.halleonard.com

ALL YOU NEED IS LOVE

FLUTE

Words and Music by JOHN LENNON
and PAUL McCARTNEY

BLACKBIRD

Flute

Words and Music by JOHN LENNON
and PAUL McCARTNEY

DAY TRIPPER

FLUTE

Words and Music by JOHN LENNON
and PAUL McCARTNEY

ELEANOR RIGBY

Flute

Words and Music by JOHN LENNON
and PAUL McCARTNEY

GET BACK

FLUTE

Words and Music by JOHN LENNON
and PAUL McCARTNEY

HERE, THERE AND EVERYWHERE

FLUTE

Words and Music by JOHN LENNON
and PAUL McCARTNEY

HEY JUDE

FLUTE

Words and Music by JOHN LENNON
and PAUL McCARTNEY

I WILL

FLUTE

Words and Music by JOHN LENNON
and PAUL McCARTNEY

LET IT BE

FLUTE

Words and Music by JOHN LENNON
and PAUL McCARTNEY

Slowly, with feeling

LUCY IN THE SKY WITH DIAMONDS

FLUTE

Words and Music by JOHN LENNON
and PAUL McCARTNEY

OB-LA-DI, OB-LA-DA

FLUTE

Words and Music by JOHN LENNON
and PAUL McCARTNEY

PENNY LANE

FLUTE

Words and Music by JOHN LENNON
and PAUL McCARTNEY

SOMETHING

FLUTE

Words and Music by
GEORGE HARRISON

TICKET TO RIDE

FLUTE

Words and Music by JOHN LENNON
and PAUL McCARTNEY

YESTERDAY

FLUTE

Words and Music by JOHN LENNON
and PAUL McCARTNEY